Watching
Kangaroos
in Australia

ouise and Richard Spilsbury

Heinemann
LIBRARY

H www.heinemann.co.uk/library

Visit our website to find out more information about Heinemann Library books.

To order:

☎ Phone 44 (0) 1865 888066

▤ Send a fax to 44 (0) 1865 314091

▯ Visit the Heinemann Bookshop at www.heinemann.co.uk/library to browse our catalogue and order online.

First published in Great Britain by Heinemann Library, Halley Court, Jordan Hill, Oxford OX2 8EJ, part of Harcourt Education. Heinemann is a registered trademark of Harcourt Education Ltd.

© Harcourt Education Ltd 2006
First published in paperback in 2007
The moral right of the proprietor has been asserted.

Editorial: Nancy Dickmann and Sarah Chappelow
Design: Ron Kamen and edesign
Illustrations: Martin Sanders
Picture Research: Maria Joannou and Christine Martin
Production: Camilla Crask
Originated by Modern Age
Printed and bound in Italy by Printer Trento srl

13 digit ISBN 978 0 431 19067 9 (HB)
10 digit ISBN 0 431 19067 4 (HB)
10 09 08 07 06
10 9 8 7 6 5 4 3 2 1

13 digit ISBN 978 0 431 19077 8 (PB)
10 digit ISBN 0 431 19077 1 (PB)
11 10 09 08 07
10 9 8 7 6 5 4 3 2 1

British Library Cataloguing in Publication Data
Spilsbury, Louise and Richard
Watching kangaroos in Australia. – (Wild world)
599.2'2217
A full catalogue record for this book is available from the British Library.

Acknowledgements
The Publishers would like to thank the following for permission to reproduce the following photographs: ANT Photolibrary pp. 20 (Tony Howard), 24 (Dick Whatford); Ardea pp. 5 (Hans & Judy Beste), 11, 15 (Jean Paul Ferrero), 19, 21 (Jean Paul Ferrero); Art Directors & TRIP p. 22 (Australian Picture Library); Corbis pp. 9 (Charles Philip Cangialosi), 14 (Theo Allofs), 18 (Martin Harvey); FLPA pp. 4 (Norbert Wu), 8 (David Hosking), 12 (Gerard Lacz), 23 (Mitsuaki Iwago), 28 (Mitsuaki Iwago); Getty Images p. 7; Lonely Planet Images p. 16 (Lawrie Williams); NHPA pp. 17 (Martin Harvey), 26 (Dave Watts); PhotoLibrary.com pp. 10 (IFA-Bilderteam Gmbh), 13 (Picture Press), 27 (Index Stock Imagery); Science Photo Library p. 25 (Art Wolfe). Cover photograph of kangaroos reproduced with permission of FLPA/ Norbert Wu.

The publishers would like to thank Michael Bright of the BBC Natural History Unit for his assistance in the preparation of this book.

Every effort has been made to contact copyright holders of any material reproduced in this book. Any omissions will be rectified in subsequent printings if notice is given to the publishers. The paper used to print this book comes from sustainable resources.

Contents

Meet the kangaroos 4

Australia's bush country 6

There's a kangaroo! 8

Land of the kangaroos 10

On the move 12

Daily life .14

Feeding time 16

Hot and dry 18

Keeping cool 20

Baby kangaroos 22

Growing up 24

Dangers 26

Tracker's guide 28

Glossary 30

Find out more 31

Index 32

Words written in bold, **like this**, are explained in the glossary.

Meet the kangaroos

This is Australia, the home of kangaroos. There are many different kinds of kangaroo. The red and grey kangaroos are the biggest and the best known.

▼ *Kangaroos live in the **bush**.*

Most kangaroos get around by hopping.
Some kinds are as small as a rabbit. Other
kinds live in trees.

▶▶ *Tree kangaroos
walk instead
of hop.*

Australia's bush country

Australia is the smallest **continent** in the world. Most kangaroos live in Australia. Some kinds live in Papua New Guinea and New Zealand.

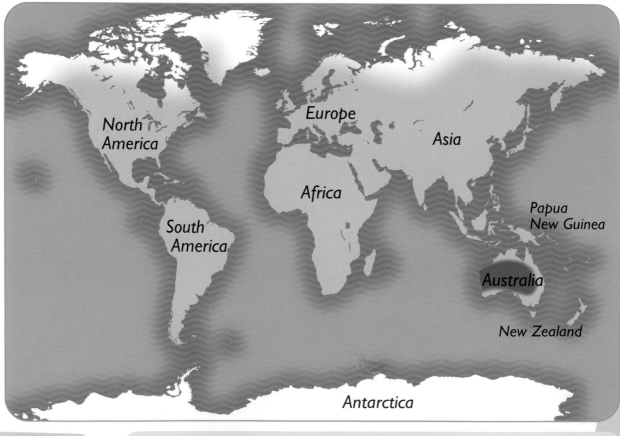

Key   ● *This colour shows where red and grey kangaroos live in Australia.*

Most kangaroos live in dry parts of Australia. This land is called **bush** country. It has many wide open spaces.

▲ *In bush country there are grass plants, a few trees, and some thorny bushes.*

There's a kangaroo!

This is a red kangaroo. Red kangaroos have short front arms and very big back legs. They have big ears and a huge tail.

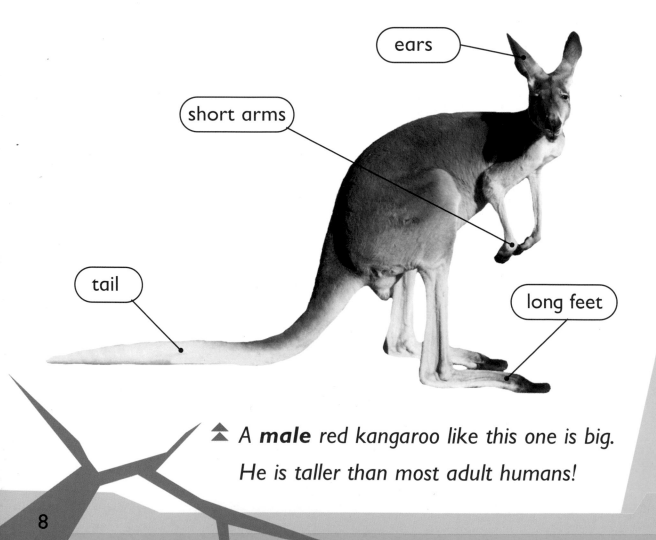

ears

short arms

tail

long feet

▲ A **male** red kangaroo like this one is big. He is taller than most adult humans!

*Young kangaroos are called **joeys**.*

This is a **female** kangaroo. She is smaller than the male. Females have a pouch on their tummy. Baby kangaroos grow and keep safe there.

Land of the kangaroos

In open **bush** country it is hard to hide. Sometimes kangaroos travel together in groups called mobs. They take turns watching out for danger.

▶▶ *These kangaroos can twist their ears to hear what is going on all around them.*

▼ *These kangaroos will stay in the same area of bush land for most of the year.*

Kangaroos can travel a long way on their big legs. They usually stay in their **home range**. This is where they live, rest, feed, and have young.

On the move

Red kangaroos move by hopping on their back legs. Across flat **bush** country they can bounce along as fast as a car. One hop can be as long as a bus.

▼ *A red kangaroo's big, strong back legs power it up and forwards through the air.*

▼ A red kangaroo cannot walk backwards. Its big tail gets in the way.

The red kangaroo's huge tail helps it to balance when it hops along. Kangaroos can also walk slowly, using their tail for balance.

Daily life

It is usually hot in the middle of the day. Many adult kangaroos are asleep. Others are **grooming**. They lick each other's fur to keep it clean.

▶▶ *Grooming is a friendly thing to do.*

The young kangaroos play while the adults sleep. They often tumble about and have boxing matches. Play fighting helps them grow strong.

◀◀ When these **male** kangaroos grow up, they may fight for real over **females**.

Feeding time

Kangaroos spend a lot of time feeding. They usually feed in the mornings and evenings.

▼ *Red kangaroos rest their short front legs on the ground as they lean forward to eat grass.*

▶▶ *Kangaroos have long, strong teeth for biting.*

Kangaroos are **herbivores**. They eat grass and other leafy plants. Their big front teeth cut the plants. Large, flat side teeth chew the food.

Hot and dry

In summer in Australia, the weather becomes very, very hot. Red kangaroos rest in the shade of trees or bushes.

▲ *Red kangaroos normally sleep when it is too hot to hop about in the sun.*

In **bush** country there is very little rain. Pools and water holes dry up. Red kangaroos **survive** if they can find grass or other leaves to eat.

▼ *These red kangaroos get the water they need from plants.*

keeping cool

Animals that live in hot places such as Australia have ways of keeping cool. Kangaroos lie down on damp mud to cool off.

▲ *This kangaroo has dug a dip in the ground to find cool earth to lie in.*

This kangaroo is licking its arms. As the water on its arms dries in the wind, it takes some of the heat away.

▶▶ *Kangaroos lick their arms to keep cool on hot days.*

Baby kangaroos

This **female** kangaroo is ready to give birth. Kangaroos are **marsupials**. A young marsupial is called a **joey**. When it is born it is only the size of a small bean.

▸▸ *This pregnant kangaroo will look after her joey for several years.*

The joey climbs up its mother's fur into her pouch. Inside the pouch, it grabs on to a **teat**. It starts to drink its mother's milk.

▲ *This tiny joey is helpless. It cannot see or hear, but it is safe inside its mother's pouch.*

Growing up

This **joey** is now four months old. Sometimes he gets out of his mother's pouch to explore. He climbs back in to feed and feel safe.

▶▶ *When joeys first leave their mother's pouch, they are a bit wobbly on their feet.*

This joey is about one year old. She stays out of her mother's pouch most of the time. She no longer drinks milk. She eats grass with the adult kangaroos.

▼ *Even big joeys still try to hop back into their mother's pouch when they get tired!*

Dangers

Some kangaroos are killed in fires. Fires spread through the dry **bush** in summer. Young kangaroos are also in danger from dingos (wild dogs found in Australia).

▼ *Dingos follow scent trails to find kangaroos.*

▶▶ *Warning signs tell people where kangaroos cross roads. This protects drivers and kangaroos.*

Many young kangaroos are hit by cars. The young kangaroos that **survive** will grow into adults. They could have **joeys** of their own in a few years.

Tracker's guide

Spotting and identifying the tracks of wild creatures is fun. Kangaroos are usually easy to spot.

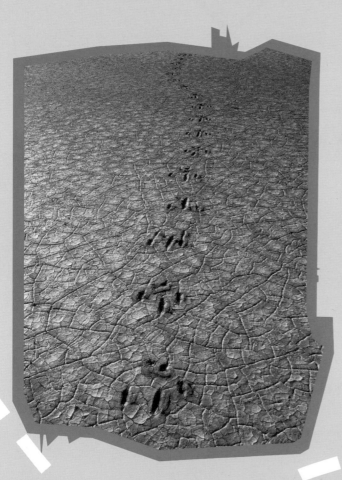

◀◀ *When kangaroos hop, they leave front and back paw prints as well as a tail print.*

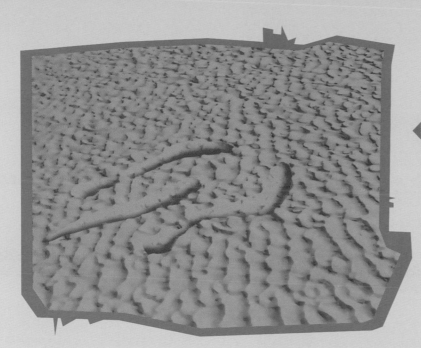

◀◀ A kangaroo also often drags its tail along the ground.

▶▶ You might also find kangaroo droppings.

Glossary

bush land that has a few trees, some bushes and grass plants growing on it. This kind of land covers a lot of Australia.

continent the world is split into seven large areas of land called continents. Each continent is divided into different countries.

female animal that can become a mother when it is grown up. Girls and women are female people.

groom lick or clean fur

herbivore animal that eats plants

home range area of land that an animal or group of animals, lives and feeds in

joey baby or young kangaroo

male animal that can become a father when it is grown up. Boys and men are male people.

marsupial kind of animal that carries its baby in a pouch while it grows

survive continue to live

teats part of a mother's body that her young drinks milk from

Find out more

Books

Continents: Australia and Oceania, M. Fox (Heinemann Library, 2002)

Life in a mob: Kangaroos, Louise and Richard Spilsbury
    (Heinemann Library, 2004)

We're from Australia, Vic Parker (Heinemann Library, 2005)

Why am I a mammal? Greg Pyers (Raintree, 2005)

Why do animals have tails? Elizabeth Miles (Heinemann Library, 2002)

Websites

Have a look at this website to find out more about these
fascinating creatures:

http://www.red-kangaroos.com/

This website has lots of amazing facts about kangaroos:

http://www.bbc.co.uk/nature/wildfacts/factfiles/643.shtml

Index

Australia 4, 6, 7, 18, 20

bush 7, 10, 11, 12, 19, 26

eating and drinking 16, 17, 19, 23, 25

fires 26

grey kangaroos 4, 5, 18, 26
grooming 14

herbivores 17
home range 11
hopping 4, 12, 13, 18, 25

joeys 9, 15, 22, 23, 24, 25, 27

licking 21

marsupials 22
mobs 10

pouches 9, 22, 23, 24, 25

tails 8, 13, 29
teats 23
teeth 17
tree kangaroos 5